Welcome to the Circus

Roll up! Roll up! 2
Stilt Walkers 4
Ringmaster 6
Jugglers 8
Trapeze Artists 10
Acrobats 12
Clowns 14
Tightrope Walkers 16
Learn to Balance 18
Paint your Face 20
Learn to Stilt Walk 22

Written by Sean Callery

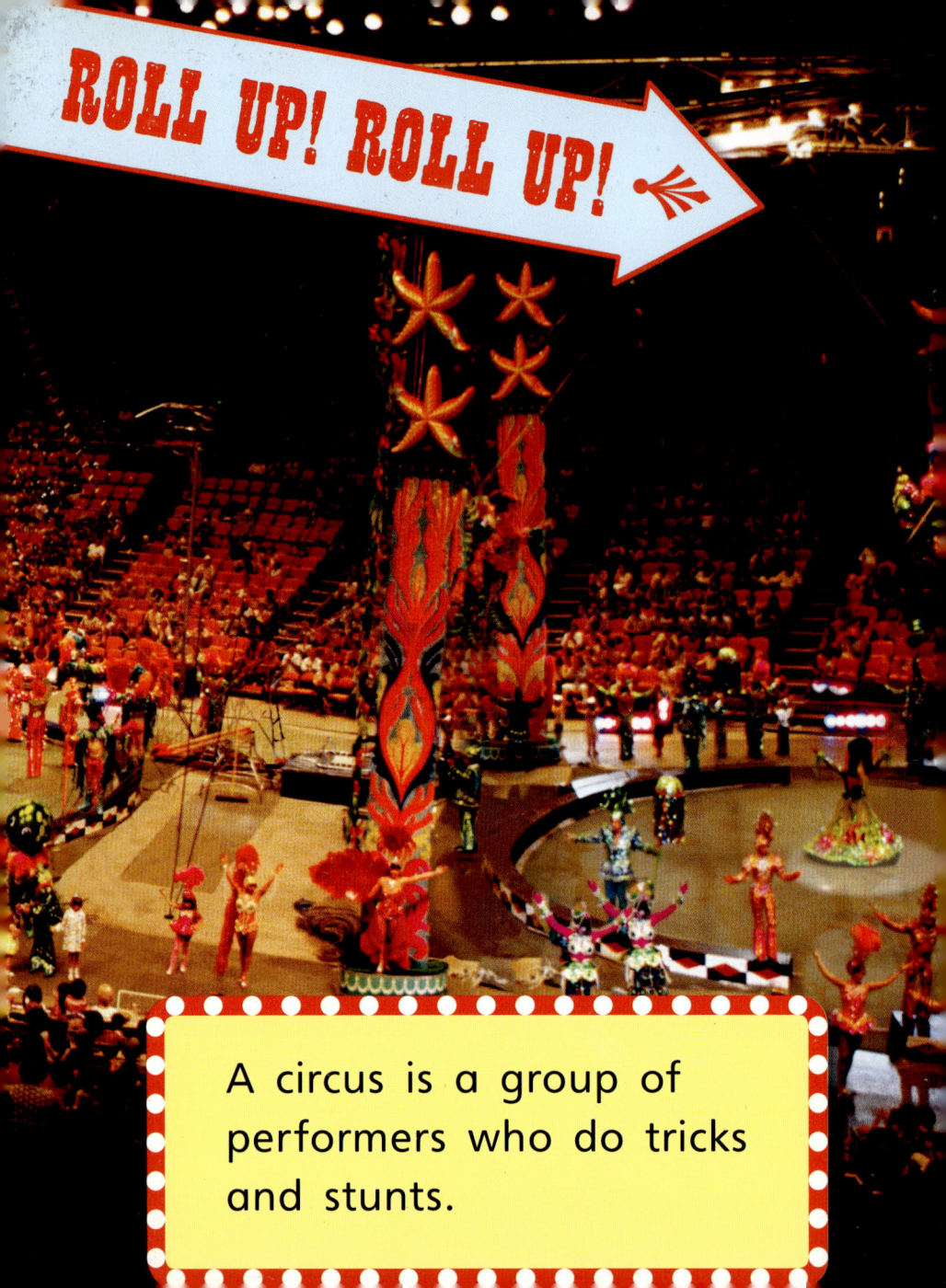

ROLL UP! ROLL UP!

A circus is a group of performers who do tricks and stunts.

They travel to different places and show off their acts in a huge tent called the Big Top. They are always on the move!

3

STILT WALKERS

Stilt walkers stand on long poles to make themselves very, very tall. They lead the circus parade and welcome the crowd to the Big Top.

The poles have special steps for the stilt walkers to stand on.

RINGMASTER

The ringmaster gets everyone to clap each new act. The ringmaster wears a bright coat and a tall hat. Sometimes he dances and sings with the performers.

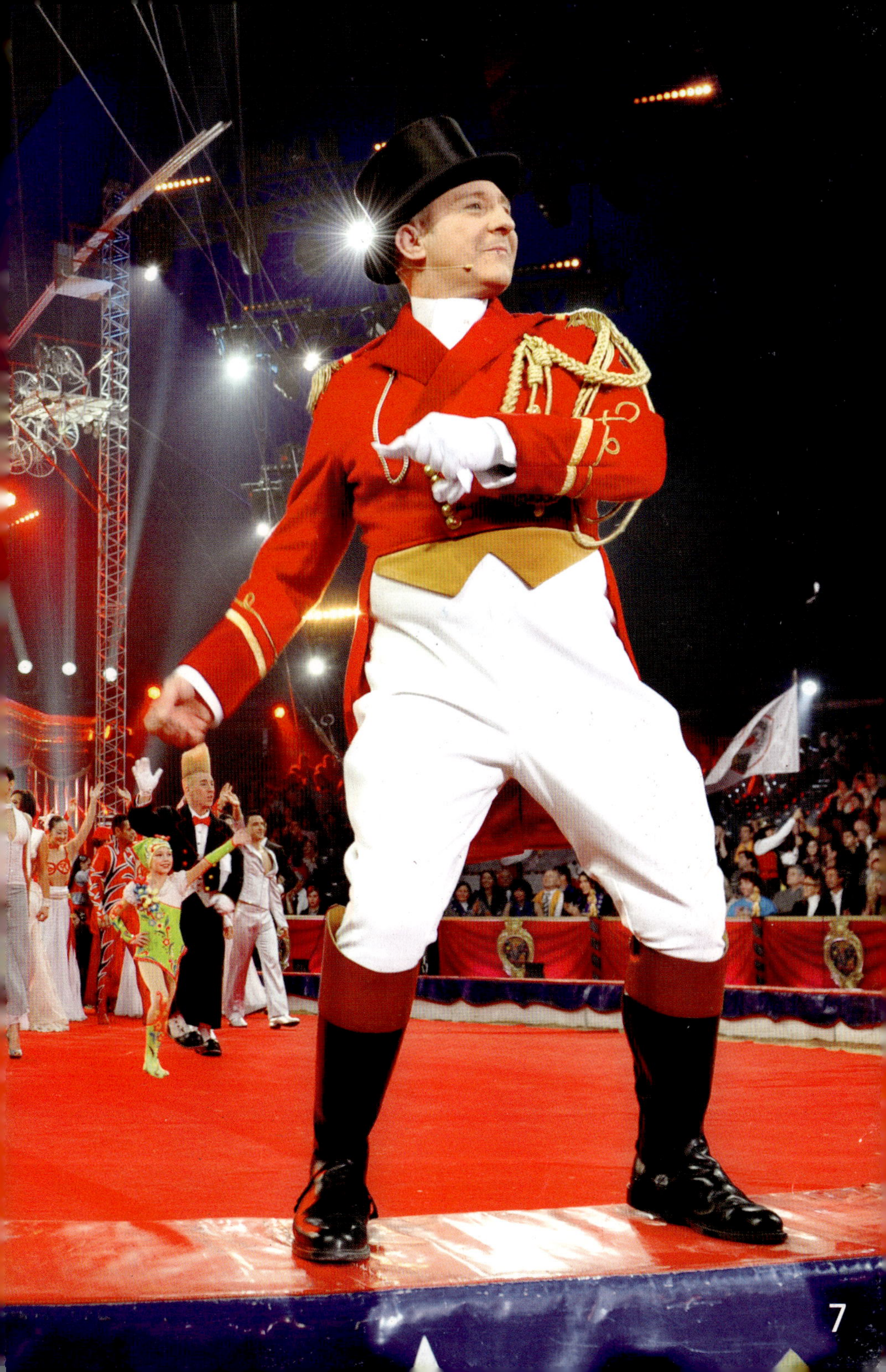

JUGGLERS

Jugglers throw balls, rings or clubs in the air and catch them. They keep lots of things in the air at the same time.

8

Sometimes jugglers work in a group and fling objects to each other very fast.

TRAPEZE ARTISTS

The trapeze is a bar like a big swing. Trapeze artists do stunts on it, high above the ground.

Sometimes they jump between two swinging bars. One might even catch another in mid-air.

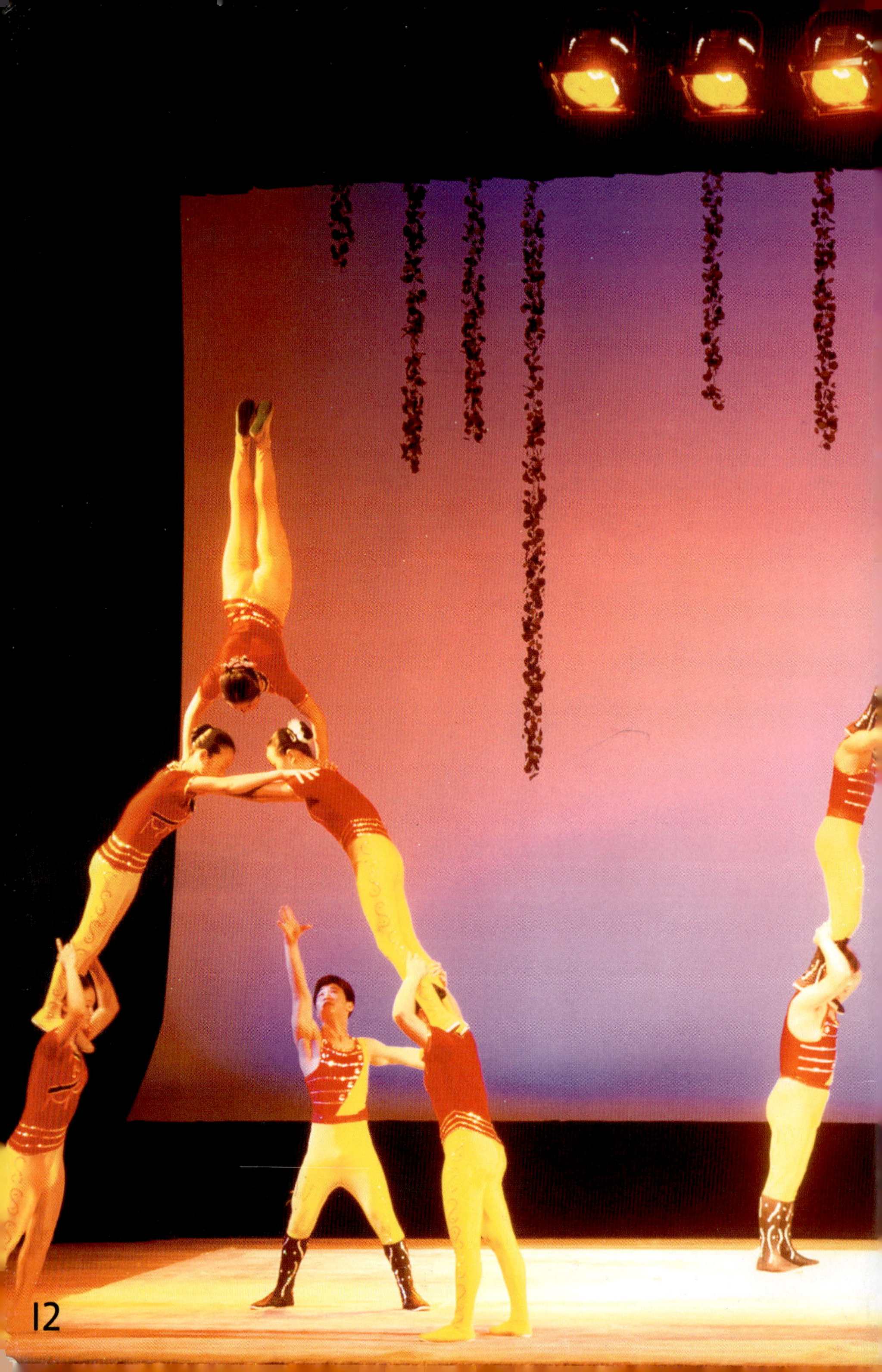

ACROBATS

Acrobats are very flexible. They can bend their bodies into amazing shapes! Sometimes they climb on each other's shoulders to balance and jump. When lots of acrobats climb up on each other, they can make a human pyramid.

CLOWNS

Clowns do funny things to make people laugh, but they never speak. They trip up, fall over and play tricks on people.

Sometimes, they juggle and do trapeze acts.

TIGHTROPE WALKERS

The tightrope is rope or thick wire stretched high above the crowd.

16

Tightrope walkers hold a long pole to help them balance while they walk along the rope. They stand on one leg, turn around and jump in the air.

17

LEARN TO BALANCE

Acrobats and tightrope walkers need to be good at balancing.

Mark a line on the ground with chalk.

Walk along it with your head up. Turn and go back.

18

Now do this with a bean bag on your head.

Balance a rolled-up sock on your foot.

How fast can you hop and keep the sock there?

19

PAINT YOUR FACE

Clowns paint their faces in different ways. Try this one with face paints:

1. Colour your face white.

2. Paint your nose red.

3. Draw in a huge smile around the outside of your mouth.

4. Use black paint around your mouth and for your eyebrows.

LEARN TO STILT WALK

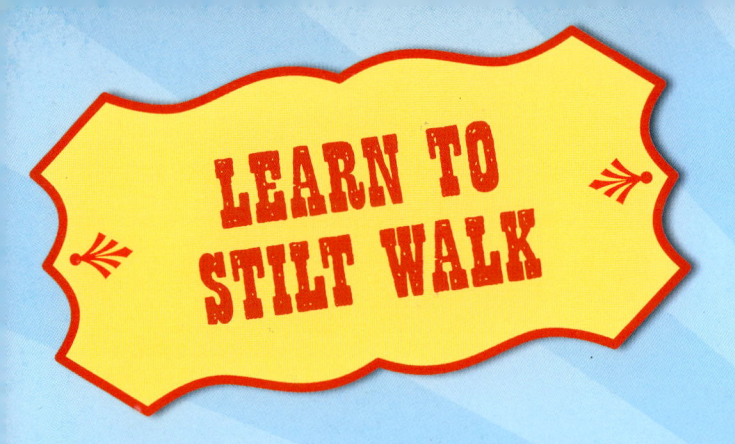

You can make your own stilts!

Use old tin cans or paint pots with string tied through holes in the sides.

Stand next to something you can lean on, like a wall, or a friend who can catch you.

It is best if you keep moving!

23

IT'S SHOWTIME!